This was a mountain....now a sand dune

Hopkins Hill Rd. West Greenwich, RI

Victor George Moffitt, author

"I used to hunt birds here with my Dad"

The birds are now gone…

Fifty year have passed and not a single drop of water has come from the Big River Reservoir Project

1

Dedicated to Etta Wood

and all the other victims of unjust Eminent Domain

especially those in Rhode Island from the Towns of

West Greenwich, East Greenwich, Coventry, and Exeter

whose land was taken, never used, and never returned.

Acknowledgments

I have been compiling information on the Big River Reservoir project for many years it was about one year ago I started writing this book.

I was inspired to dedicate this book to Etta Wood whom I've personally known for many years as a client and friend. Her personal story and interview will always be close to my heart.

Other Big River familes who land was seized were also instrumental in motivating me to write this book…as someone needed to write it for them.

Ian Longren a former URI student who completed a term paper on the subject, I provided him various information, helped me in the early on with organizing layout and materials.

Robert Morris helped me put all my data into an organized format and the concept of decades was created.

Finally, my son Brian Moffitt performed a miracle by editing, formatting text and adding pictures to my unfinished work to help put the finishing touches on the book.

I also want to personally thank the Providence Journal staff and their writers who over the past 50 years have presented Rhode Islanders with many stories, details and investigative reports about the Big River Reservoir project.

Table of Contents

Foreword

Our United States Constitution was carefully designed to protect American citizens from governmental abuse and guarantee individual rights. When we neglect individuals whose constitutional rights have been violated and do nothing, we are no better than the unjust government that failed its citizens in the first place. And then, when that same government returns under false pretenses with its hand out to take our property as well, who will protect us?

Over the past 50 years Rhode Island has survived the so called water shortage.

In 1929 the Scituate reservoir was completed that supplies over 41 billion gallons and except for only two short period of drought, has supplied adequate water for more than half of all Rhode Islanders for the past 50 years.

As I record this true story from the small State of Rhode Island and Providence Plantations, here we are in 2014 the 50th anniversary of the 1964 confiscation of the property for the proposed "Big River Reservoir". In 1964 I was 14 years old and was attending the West Greenwich Elementary School; I personally knew many of the people who were affected by this violation of their constitutional rights. That is why I have always been and always will be fighting for them. Many have passed away over the last fifty years but their next of kin should have their family's land returned to them as it is never too late to right a wrong. That is my purpose for writing this book.

After all these years the land sits unused. Any proposals to return the land to the rightful owners have been rejected by the state government, and no substantial proposal for alternate use has been approved. Consequently, over 8000 acres of prime real estate sits idle and unproductive, a shameful monument to government waste and abuse.

This is a story of Big Brother Government namely the State of Rhode Island and Providence Plantations, forcing a small farming community out of their homes for a "Reservoir" that was never, and now clearly will never, be built. The facts you will learn regarding this project are so alarming you may very well doubt this could happen in America.

As you read through this book and discover the facts, I hope it will make you as angry and frustrated as I am. Perhaps by working together we can ensure such injustice is never done again, and we can create a "happy ending" for those families that **Eminent Domain – Violated**!

ALL PROFITS FROM THIS BOOK WILL BE DONATED TO THE BIG RIVER FAMILIES LEGAL FUND

Chapter 1
The People: Why Should We Care?

Etta M. Wood with author
Victor Moffitt

I recently visited with Etta M. Wood a former resident of West Greenwich whose property was taken by the Big River Reservoir project and this is what she had to say.

Etta is now 96 years old (she was born July 30, 1918) and currently living at the Woodpecker Hill nursing facility in Greene (Coventry), Rhode Island. She recalls buying 30 acres of land on New London Turnpike in West Greenwich in 1963 with her husband Henry N. Wood, Jr. and their children to build a new home and horse farm. She purchased the land from Mr. Little a real estate agent from East Greenwich, RI. It took several years to clear the land and build the house and barn. The couples life ambition was for filled to build a beautiful new home, barn and raise horses for the children. Life was wonderful until the State of Rhode Island decided to build a reservoir in the Big River area. The Wood family along with 239 other families was forced to sell and relocate. When I asked Etta how that made her feel, she said, *"It messed up our life and we didn't know what we were going to do"*. Etta and her family eventually found and purchased land in Foster, Rhode Island. They were allowed to rent their former home for several years until they hired Ocean State Movers to move their house from West Greenwich to Foster. Etta's husband Henry however never totally recovered from the stress of moving and losing their dream home and died several years later after moving to Foster. I asked Etta if her property was not taken for the reservoir project where her family would live today and she answered, *"We would certainly still be living in our beautiful home in West Greenwich."* Etta had previously presented me with a file folder of original documents from that time frame regarding the eminent domain land seizure for the proposed Big River Reservoir project. Some of the documents she gave me were the official act Chapter 133, Public Laws 1964 JANUARY SESSION, 1964; state of Rhode Island and Providence Plantations Water Resources Coordinating Board (land description) signed by Walter J. Shea, Chairman of the WRCB on January 31st 1966 (19 pages) and several documents pertaining to a suit regarding property values vis the Water Resources Coordinating Board hereafter known as WRCB.

Etta and Henry had to sue the WRCB and hire experienced real estate agents to value their property. They hired Henry C. Hoxsie, real estate broker from West Greenwich and Ugo S. Garganese, real estate agent of Regent Realty from Warwick to evaluate their property. The WRCB hired Mr. DiPrete. The valuations are shown in Table 1.

Table 1 Appraised Values of the Wood Family Property

Appraiser	Appraised Value
Mr. Hoxsie	$51,400.00
Mr. Garganese	$46,970.00
Mr. DiPrete	$33,000.00

The court finds that on the date of condemnation, this property was worth $42,000.00.

The original offer by the WRCB was only $30,000.00.

Etta and Henry had to pay out from their proceeds attorney fees $4,351.76 **and** appraisal fees or $650.00. The defendants did agree to pay additional interest to the Wood's in the amount of $5,336.25. Etta could not determine or remember the total cost of the house, barn and improvements to the property as Henry did a lot of the work himself...but both monetary and emotional losses were sustained!

The preceding true story was only one of many. I have personally talked to many other previous land owners and their next of kin and stories of threats, low valuations, harassments, etc. have been stated many times.

Below is a partial listing of families and companies who land was taken per Big River land description recorded January 31, 1966 signed by Walter J Shea, Chairman of the Water Resources Coordinating Board – West Greenwich deed book 25, page 42 and duly recorded by town clerk. Deed description prepared by Charles A Maguire & Associates.

Tiogue Investment Co., Inc.

Joseph Piasczyk

Spencer MacDonald

Charles Whipple

Richard Spencer

John & Virginia Jackson

Grant Kettelle

Elizabeth Danaker

Doris Sutcliffe

Phillip Lillibridge

Albert Russell

Howard Barber

Myrtle Kettelle

James Thibault

Louis Pagliarini

Thomas Harrop

James Albro

Anne Rathbun

Russell Franklin

Albert Ferrands

Mary Sano *

Ernest Bugnot *

Raymond Moriarty

Bradford Kenyon

Additional names of landowners taken from assessors maps are as follows:

Howard C. Barbour

Roger C. Leville

Thomas E. Harrop

Ferdinando Palumbo

Robert Rathbun

Myrtle M. Kettelle

Richard Rathbun

Jerome P. & Thelma A. Duffy

George F. Searle

Henry N. Jr. & Etta M. Wood

George F. Shaw

Michael F. Sundelin

Carroll H. Green

Norman Carpentier

Philip Powers

Joseph Piaczyk

Stanley P. & Hazel Rybka

Cora W. Turner

Frank & Mary Altieri

Albina Rathbun

John Albro & Mildred Parker

Wallace E. Albro

James J. Iuliano & James E. Murphy

Howard Albro

Herman Rusack

John Rantman

Mildred Parker

Edna Dupre

Waite Albro

Thurston Albro

Clifton H. Barbour

Louis Pagliarini

James Thibault

And several other families not named here...

Big River - 7,181.6 acres of land taken

30% of the Town of West Greenwich gone

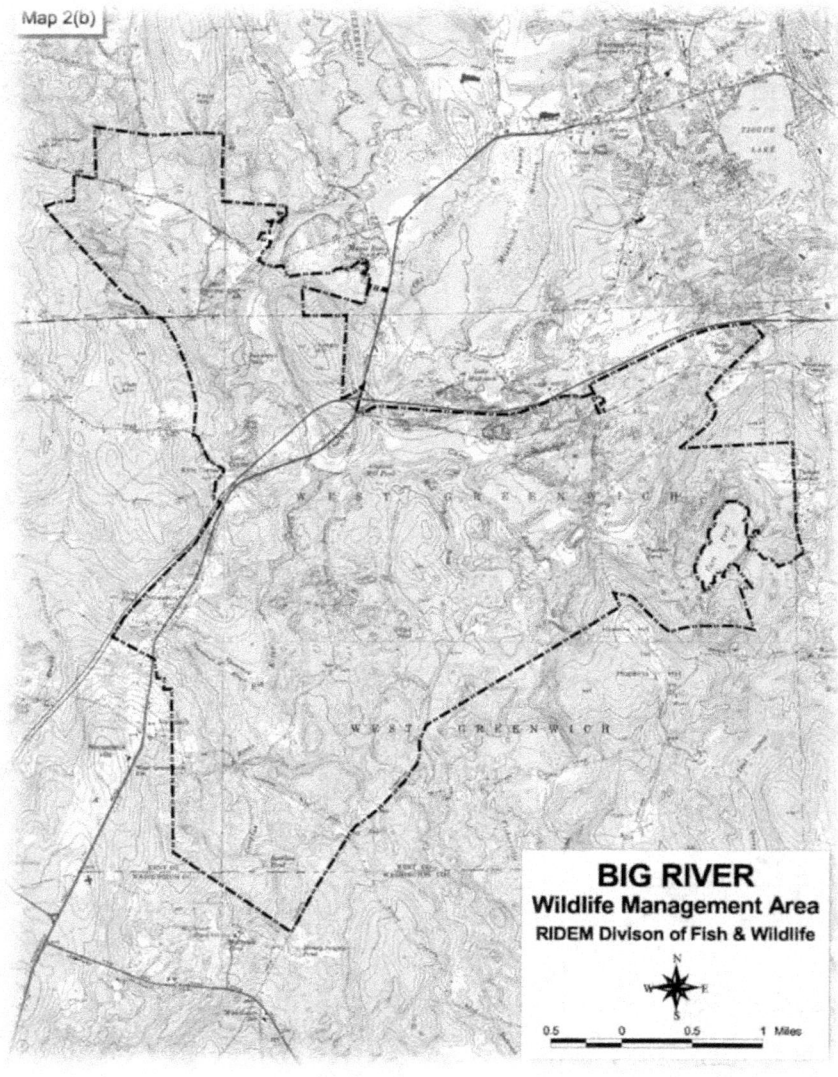

Chapter 2
Eminent Domain: Definition, Purpose and Abuses

Although a government is not a physical entity but a person or group of persons granted the power to make certain decisions, it is convenient, if not altogether necessary, that its members have a physical space in which to work. From the majestic castles of the Middle Ages, to the stoic administrative buildings of modern governance, most people take it for granted that governments must have buildings from which to wield their power.

There are other physical manifestations of this intangible concept we call government. Roads are a prime example, and, of course, military installations. The land for this critical infrastructure must come from somewhere, and it follows that there must be a mechanism for a government to acquire that land, even if individual landowners object. This mechanism we call Eminent Domain.

Eminent Domain

A right of a government to take private property for public use by virtue of the superior dominion of the sovereign power over all lands within its jurisdiction.

Source:http://www.merriam-webster.com/dictionary/eminent%20domain

The Fifth Amendment to the US Constitution provides that "private property [shall not] be taken for public use without just compensation.[1]" The Fourteenth Amendment added the requirement of just compensation to state and local government takings. The Bill of Rights (First 10 amendments to the US Constitution) contains an enumeration of rights held by individuals and states that the federal government may not abridge. The Fifth Amendment, then, recognizes two rights, and attempts to balance them. There is the right of a property owner to be secure in his property, and the right of the government to acquire land as necessary for its operation.

The following background information is provided from Wikipedia:

The Fifth Amendment to the US Constitution

The practice of condemnation was transplanted into the American colonies with the common law. In the early years, unimproved land could be taken without compensation; this practice was accepted because land was so abundant that it could be cheaply replaced. When it came time to draft the United States Constitution, differing views on eminent domain were voiced. Thomas Jefferson favored eliminating all remnants of feudalism, and pushed for allodial ownership. James Madison, who wrote the Fifth Amendment to the United States Constitution, had a more moderate view, and struck a compromise that sought to at least protect property

---

1   US Constitution, 5th Amendment

rights somewhat by explicitly mandating compensation and using the term "public use" rather than "public purpose," "public interest", or "public benefit".

The Fifth Amendment imposes limitations on the exercise of eminent domain: the taking must be for public use and just compensation must be paid. Some historians have suggested that these limitations on the taking power were inspired by the need to permit the army to secure mounts, fodder and provisions from local ranchers and the perceived need to assure them compensation for such takings. Similarly, soldiers forcibly sought housing in whatever homes were near their military assignments. To address the latter problem, the Third Amendment was enacted in 1791 as part of the US Constitution's Bill of Rights. It provided that the quartering of soldiers on private property could not take place in peacetime without the landowner's consent. It also required that, in wartime, established law had to be followed in housing troops on private property. Presumably, this would mandate "just compensation," a requirement for the exercise of eminent domain in general per the Fifth Amendment. All U.S. states have legislation specifying eminent domain procedures within their respective territories.

The power of governments to take private real or personal property has always existed in the United States, as it was once claimed to be an inherent attribute of sovereignty. This power reposes in the legislative branch of the government and may not be exercised unless the legislature has authorized its use by statutes that specify who may use it and for what purposes. The legislature may take private property by passing an Act transferring title to the government. The property owner may then seek compensation by suing in the U.S. Court of

Federal Claims. The legislature may also delegate the power to private entities like public utilities or railroads, and even to individuals for the purpose of acquiring access to their landlocked land. Its use was limited by the Takings Clause in the Fifth Amendment to the U.S. Constitution in 1791, which reads, "... nor shall private property be taken for public use, without just compensation." The Fifth Amendment did not create the national government's right to use the eminent domain power, it simply limited it to public use.

The U.S. Supreme Court has consistently deferred to the right of states to make their own determinations of public use. In 1832 the Supreme Court ruled that eminent domain could be used to allow a mill owner to expand his dam and operations by flooding an upstream neighbor. The court opinion stated that a public use does not have to mean public occupation of the land; it can mean a public benefit. In Clark vs. Nash (1905), the Supreme Court acknowledged that different parts of the country have unique circumstances and the definition of public use thus varied with the facts of the case. It ruled a farmer could expand his irrigation ditch across another farmer's land (with compensation), because that farmer was entitled to "the flow of the waters of the said Fort Canyon Creek ... and the uses of the said waters ... [is] a public use." Here, in recognizing the arid climate and geography of Utah, the Court indicated the farmer not adjacent to the river had as much right as the farmer who was, to access the waters. However, until the 14th Amendment was ratified in 1868, the limitations on eminent domain specified in the Fifth Amendment applied only to the federal government and not to the states. That view ended in 1896 when in the Chicago, Burlington & Quincy Railroad v. Chicago case the court held that the eminent domain provisions of the Fifth Amendment were incorporated in the Due Process Clause of the Fourteenth Amendment and thus were now binding on the states, or in other words, when the states take private property they are required to devote it to a public use and compensate the property owner for his loss. This was the beginning of what is now known as the "selective incorporation" doctrine.

An expansive interpretation of eminent domain was reaffirmed in Berman v. Parker (1954), in which the U.S. Supreme Court reviewed an effort by the District of Columbia to take and raze blighted structures, in order to eliminate slums in the Southwest Washington area. After the taking, held the court, the taken and razed land could be transferred to private redevelopers who would construct condominiums, private office buildings and a shopping center. The Supreme Court ruled against the owners of a non-blighted property within the area on the grounds that the project should be judged on its plans as a whole, not on a parcel by parcel basis. In Hawaii Housing Authority v. Midkiff (1984), the Supreme Court approved the use of eminent domain to transfer a land lessor's title to its tenants who owned and occupied homes built on the leased land. The court's justification was to break up a housing oligopoly, and thereby lower or stabilize home prices, although in reality, following the Midkiff decision, home prices on Oahu escalated dramatically, more than doubling within a few years.

The Supreme Court's decision in Kelo v. City of New London, 545 U.S. 469 (2005) affirmed the authority of New London, Connecticut, to take non-blighted private property by eminent domain, and then transfer it for a dollar a year to a private developer solely for the purpose of increasing municipal revenues. This 5-4 decision received heavy press coverage and inspired a public outcry criticizing eminent domain powers as too broad. In reaction to Kelo, several states enacted or are considering state legislation that would further define and restrict the power of eminent domain. The Supreme Courts of Illinois, Michigan (County of Wayne v. Hathcock [2004]), Ohio (Norwood, Ohio v. Horney [2006]), Oklahoma, and South Carolina have recently ruled to disallow such takings under their state constitutions.

The redevelopment in New London, the subject of the Kelo decision, proved to be a failure and as of 2012 (seven years after the court's decision) nothing has been built on the taken land in spite of the expenditure of over $80 million in public funds. The Pfizer corporation, which owned a $300 million research facility in the area, and would have been the primary beneficiary of the additional development, announced in 2009 that it would close its facility, and did so shortly before the expiration of its 10-year tax abatement agreement with the city. The facility was subsequently purchased in 2010 for just $55 million by General Dynamics Electric Boat.

Compensation: American courts have held that the preferred measure of "just compensation" is "fair market value," i.e., the price that a willing but unpressured buyer would pay a willing but unpressured seller in a voluntary transaction, with both parties fully informed of the property's good and bad features. Also, this approach takes into account the property's highest and best use (i.e., its most profitable use) which is not necessarily its current use or the use mandated by current zoning if there is a reasonable probability of zone change.

This measure of compensation has been severely criticized because it omits from consideration a variety of incidental economic losses that a taking of land inflicts on its owners when they are evicted from their homes and businesses. The most egregious example of such uncompensated losses is provided by the American law that denies any compensation to owners of businesses that are destroyed when land on which they are located is taken, and the business cannot relocate. A small minority of states have provided by statute that at least some business losses are compensable.

Also, attorneys' and appraisers' fees are not recoverable (except in Florida) so the owners of the taken property never recover the full value of the taken land, even if they prevail in the valuation trial, because a part of their recovery must be used to pay their lawyers and appraisers. Some states do provide for limited recovery of such litigation expenses, typically when the owners' recovery substantially exceeds the amount of the condemner's pretrial offer or the evidence presented by the contemnor at trial by a specified percentage. Also, when a condemnation action is abandoned, the owners are typically entitled (by statute) to be paid reasonable attorneys' and appraisers' fee they had to incur in defending the condemnation action while it was pending.

When payment of compensation is delayed, the owner of the taken land is entitled to receive interest on the award of compensation that accrues from the time of taking to the time of payment.

The interest must be reasonable, so that when prevailing market rates of interest exceed the statutory rate (as in inflationary times), the former have to be used.

The U.S. Supreme Court takes the position that unlike the determination of what is a "public use," the determination of compensation is a judicial, not legislative, function, but legislatures are free to provide for more liberal awards of compensation than the constitutional minimum determined by courts.

In cases of partial takings of land, the owners are entitled to compensation for the taken part, plus severance damages (the diminution of value of what remains of their property after the taking). If the partial taking creates special benefits (i.e., it causes an increase in the value of the remaining land) their value is offset against compensation, with the majority of states allowing such offsets only against severance damages, so in those states, the owner always gets paid for the taken land. When a partial taking causes impairment of access to the remainder land, that gives rise to a contentious issue because courts take the position that diminution in value caused by impaired access is compensable only when the impairment is substantial. Traffic regulations that affect access (one-way streets, median dividers, etc.) are deemed exercises of the police power and are not compensable.

In addition to fee simple titles, all interests in property (easements, leaseholds, etc.) are compensable. The measure of value of a leasehold is the amount by which prevailing comparable rentals in the area exceed the actual contracted-for rent. This amount is known as "bonus value" of a lease. It is calculated over the remaining life of the lease and then reduced to its present value. The measure of compensation for an easement is the difference in the value of the subject land as unencumbered and as encumbered by the easement.

In determining value, zoning and other land-use regulations are considered, but if it appears that there is a reasonable probability of zone change to a higher use, that may be shown and in that case the owner is entitled to an additional increment of value (the extra amount over and above the value under current zoning, that the market would pay now because of the probability of future rezoning).

The appraisal profession recognizes several different methods of calculating value, but courts are largely stuck in the convention of using three valuation approaches: (a) market data analysis or comparable sales value, (b) the capitalization of rentals, and (c) the reproduction-less-depreciation approach under which the cost of reproducing the improvements on the property is estimated and then depreciated to allow for wear and tear and functional or economic obsolescence. The value of the land is then added to the value of the reproduced, depreciated improvements. Some states allow compensation as the cost of reproduction without depreciation, but only in cases where the subject property, though privately owned, performs an important public or charitable function.

The U.S. Supreme Court has indicated (U.S. v. Cors) that it is not its intention to make a "fetish" out of market value as the measure of compensation, and that other approaches may be used when conventional methods do not work, or if applied, would create an injustice (Pewee Coal v. United States). But this appears to be a hortatory, rather than doctrinal statement. These situations, however, are extremely rare.

Studies in several parts of the country (California, Georgia, Minnesota, New York and Utah) have demonstrated that condemning agencies frequently undercompensate property owners, and that those owners who reject the pre-litigation offers and go to court tend to recover substantially higher awards, whether by judges or juries.

The preceding are examples that represent cases of eminent domain that were settled within a reasonable time, but in the state of Rhode Island and Providence Plantations fifty years is not long enough!!

We will now continue with the story…

Government taking of land is common in America, and the process generally follows the same pattern:

1. Condemnation
   The acquiring agency [who would that be?] passes a resolution to take the property, including a declaration of public need. This condemnation is distinct from declaring a property blighted.

2. Appraisal

   An ostensibly independent appraiser will estimate the value of the property.

3. Offer and negotiation

   There may be several rounds of negotiation before a homeowner is satisfied. Or not.

4. Lawsuit

If a landowner is not satisfied with the government's final offer, he may sue the acquiring agency for better (more 'just') compensation. The government, however, generally becomes owner while a trial is pending, and the amount of the offer deposited in a trust account. This suit is almost never about the right to take the land (that is too well established) but is solely intended to increase the compensation.

In order for this process to take place, the government must intend some 'Public Use'. This term is not well defined, but may include any of the following:

1. Schools
2. Roads and highways
3. Parks
4. Airports
5. Dams
6. Reservoirs
7. Redevelopment
8. Public housing
9. Hospitals
10. Public buildings

One thing conspicuously absent from the list, as we will discuss later, is "**open space**".

Eminent domain law was never intended to take private property namely land and use it for "open space".

Tarbox Pond, Hopkins Hill Road
West Greenwich
Located within Big RiverArea

Chapter 3 – Decade of the 1950's
Big River Beginnings

The 1950's

- Potential reservoir sites identified

- Poor projections were made on expected water consumption, especially for industrial use (that never materialized!)

- Population projections were overstated to imply future water shortages

- Geological surveys and engineering studies were not completed prior to Eminent Domain seizure

Though I take this Big River Reservoir topic very seriously, let me add a humorous anecdote for you:

FYI: I was born on February 2, 1950, so that makes me an **Aquarian groundhog**. As you know Aquarians are "water bearers" so that is my connection to "reservoirs'.

Ok…now back to the story…

In 1952, Charles A. Maguire & Associates, engineering consultants, were hired by the Rhode Island Water Resources Commission to prepare a study of available sites for a potential reservoir in the State of Rhode Island. They compiled a list of seven potential sites. The list included the Big River Reservoir, the Chepachet River Reservoir, the Clear River Reservoir, the Nipmuck River Reservoir, the Nooseneck River Reservoir, the Oak Valley River Reservoir and the Smith-Sayles-Keech Reservoir, The proposed sites are a combination of expansions of existing reservoirs and new construction that would cost over 25 million with an estimated yield of about 100 million gallon daily.

Table 2 summarizes the estimated reservoir cost and estimated safe yields in terms of millions of daily gallons.

Table 2 Estimated Reservoir Costs and Safe Yields

Reservoir Name	Estimated Cost	Estimated Daily Gallons (millions)
Big River	$3,720,000	37.8
Chepachet River	2,960,000	18.1
Clear River	12,020,000	9.6
Nipmuck River	2,360,000	14.7
Nooseneck River	2,000,000	7.1
Oak Valley	2,800,000	6.3
Smith-Sayles-Keech	620,000	6.9
TOTALS	$25,480,000	100.5

The following are quotes found within the study:

"The future prosperity of the State of Rhode Island is, in our opinion, dependent to a large extent on expansion of the state's industrial activity and to a lesser degree on recreational activities."

"Many industries require large quantities of water for processing and in many instances; these large supplies cannot be economically made available at the site of the industry."

Accordingly, any program of industrial expansion in the

State of Rhode Island must recognize the necessity of further development of the surface and ground water sources of the state, either by industry or through the assistance of a state development board or commission.

"We believe that careful examination of the various possibilities of reservoir construction with any planning programs by the state agencies."

In 1958 the engineering firm of Metcalf and Eddy predicted the "Big River" reservoir project would cost $22.7 million (phase II only). State officials said at that time they wanted the reservoir completed by 1968 **AT THE LATEST!**

A Providence Journal article written on January 6, 1958 regarding seven proposed reservoir sites, estimated the cost for the Big River reservoir would be about $5,011,200. In that same article per capita water consumption was estimated to be 110 gallons per day based upon 1956 population of 838,000. Based upon a projected 2001 population of 1,255,000, 150 gallons per day would be needed – a shortfall of about 30 million gallons per day.

One of the Last Remaining Businesses on the Original Land Seized for Big River (Owners Must Pay Rent to Continue Operating).

Chapter 4 – Decade of the 1960's
The Project Falters, But Begins

In January, 1960 the late Governor Christopher Del Sesto in his annual budget message to the General Assembly proposed the state approve enough money to purchase 11,856 acres of land around the Big River and Wood River to construct two reservoirs that would yield about 60 million gallons of water needed for reserves to meet growing demand of the state's suburbs.

Soon after the Governor's message opposition surfaced. West Greenwich officials warned 60% of their town revenues would be lost and how would they pay for a new school they were building and complained that their town would cease to exist. Others asked state to consider pumping ground water or even desalinating sea water as an alternative. The General Assembly killed the 1st bond issue before it even went to the voters.

In 1962, a severe drought occurred and water reserves

were very low so the General Assembly finally approved a bonding referendum that the voters later rejected 95,915 to 65,603.

Two years later in 1964 the General Assembly revised its bond issue for $5 million to buy land for Big River. Only that was approved by the voters.

January Session, 1962 – Chapter 91

An ACT to provide for the authority to issue bonds and notes to finance the acquisition of sites for RESEVOIRS for public water supply (5 million dollar bond)

The ACT granted power to enter into leases and agreements not exceeding 20 years.

The ACT granted exemption from local taxation reduced by 4% per year for 25 years.

In 1962 Rhode Island voters rejected the 5 million bond issue for Big River.

In 1964 Rhode Island voters approved the 5 million bond issue for Big River.

Note: H 1624 approved on April 30, 1964

Landowner names listed in land description H 1624:

James Thibault, Robert Rathbun estate, Myrtle Kettelle, Howard C. Barbour, Albert I. Russell, Phillip Lillibridge, Norma Kinne, Kent County Water authority, ElizaBETH d. Daneker, John W. Jackson, Albert Spencer,

Charles Whipple, Spencer Kent McDonald, Freeman Boutilier, Alfred R. & Helen R. Chatelle, Leslie S. & Geraldine W. Daly, Robert G. Dunbar, Arnold A. & Doris Weeden, Michael Fitzpatrick, Harold F. & Beryl E. Potter, John J. Murphy, F. G. Matullo, John R. Hinkley, George, Arthur & Angelo Manni, Lester Phillips, Earl L. Jordan, John & Rose Assalone, George & Anna Roberts, Charles R. Healey, Elmer J. Rathbun, Bradford H. Kenyon, Raymond Moriarity, E. Bugnet, Howard C. Baker, John H. Potter, Rolf H. Kroekel, Arthur R. Palmgren, Mary J. Sepe, Louis Faria, Stanley & Anna Sowens, Russell Franklin, Houghton Metcalf,

Containing 8,623 acres more or less, all shown on that certain plan entitled "Preliminary plan of proposed Big river reservoir project, Coventry, West Greenwich, East Greenwich, and Exeter, Rhode Island, Charles A. Maguire & Associates, engineers, September 24, 1959, revised, April, 1961". The act was attested by then Secretary of State August LaFrance.

In 1965, the late Gov. John Chafee gave the approval for condemning the land.

In 1968, an additional $2.5 million was approved to purchase the remaining condemned land in the Big River.

In 1969, the late Gov. Frank Licht decided to let the Water Supply Board develop the reservoir if it could work out an agreement to buy the land from the state. More delays and NO construction!!

Chapter 5 – Decade of the 1970's
Bureaucracy, Delays, Problems Arise

The 1970's

- **Various bond issues defeated by RI voters**

- **Another decade passes with NO designs and NO construction!**

Throughout the 1970's various bond issues to build the Big River Reservoir were defeated by Rhode Island voters.

In July of 1971, the late Providence Major Joseph A. Doorley, Jr. killed all proposals of the Water Supply Board to purchase Big River property cited numerous issues of state regulations. Back to square one... but still NO construction.

In 1974, an advisory council to the state Department of Natural Resources urged the state to use for wildlife and recreation the 8,600 acres it had acquired for Big River. The council cited the project, and then estimated cost of $60 million would mean increased water use, sewage flow and pollution. However, the late Gov. Philip W. Noel insisted it should be built and sought $3 million to begin designs. Voters did not agree and rejected the proposed bond issue.

In 1975, Providence Mayor Vincent A."Buddy" Cianci, Jr. asked the General Assembly to add representatives from outlying communities to the Water Supply Board to booster support for the Big River reservoir project. The legislature refused and the plan died.

In 1976, the late Gov. J. Joseph Garrahy pushed the project requesting the Army Corps of Engineers to build Big River. The Corps proposed a $70 million project but that project was dropped against angry public reactions. The US Army Corp of Engineers sited numerous problems with the proposed reservoir.

In 1976 and 1978, engineering bond issues were both rejected by voters.

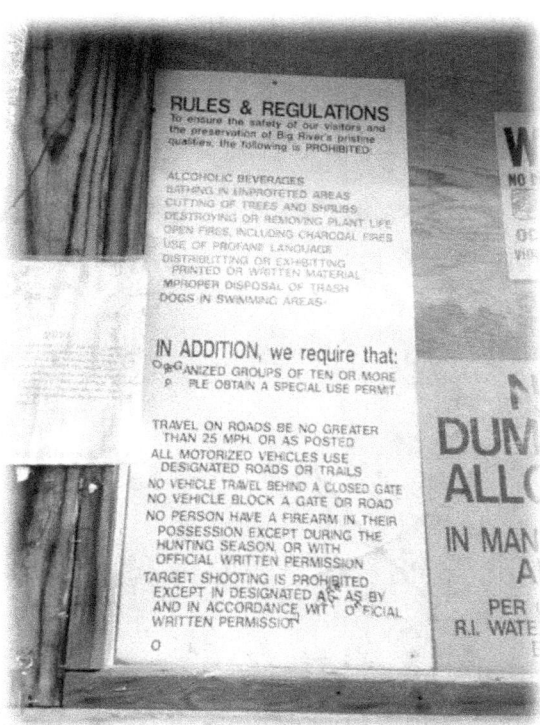

Chapter 6 – Decade of the 1980's
EPA Kills the Project

The 1980's

- Federal aid for the project is cancelled.

- Big Reservoir project DEAD!!! R.I.P.

Several interesting articles were written in the Providence Journal during the 1980's. I recommend readers who want more detailed information to go to the Providence Journal archives regarding the Big River project.

On April 30, 1989 the Providence Journal wrote an investigative article regarding the State selling sand and gravel dirt-cheap to some local construction companies without requiring them to use the normal bidding process. The article uncovered that contractors paid 20 cents a cubic yard for the same material that they would have cost them up to $6 or more elsewhere. As least one contractor sold the material for 7 to 12 times more than he paid. Such "scalping" violates an agreement with the water resources board.

The State has bought back its own sand from one Big River contractor, Cardi Corp. of Warwick. Cardi processed and delivered sand to the Department of Transportation for about 27 times the price it originally paid. The board allowed the contractors to calculate the amounts of sand and gravel they removed. Billing was done on the honor system. Digging actually started in 1972. During that 16 years period of digging, contractors removed about 6.5 million cubic yards of sand and gravel. Excavation has turned a preserve of white pines into a strip-mined desert.

In 1987, the water resource board using its own monies completed some engineering work and part of the environmental studies.

Estimated cost to build Big River Reservoir:

1958 = $22.7 million

1989 = $282 million

Current = ???

In 1989 the Environmental Protection Agency (EPA) turned down Federal 404c funding for the proposed Big River Reservoir project citing several factors: poor location because Interstate 95 crosses 2,500 ft. of the proposed reservoir and four miles of the proposed watershed, construction would reduce freshwater flow into the Pawtuxet River, construction would destroy 550 acres of irreplaceable wetlands and 3,000 acres of pristine forest. The proposed reservoir would displace 221 species of birds, 55 species of mammals, 37 species or reptiles and amphibians, including species on an endangered list.

There is absolutely no hope that the environmental reasons precluding construction over the past 27 years (1962 – 1989) will ever change in the future. In fact, on September 27, 1990, the United States House of Representations passed legislation canceling Congressional authorization of federal aid for the Big River Reservoir Project.

The EPA believes insofar as the Big River project provides benefits of flood control and recreation, which could be achieved through less environmentally damaging measures. The EPA further indicated that 5-10 MGD (Million Gallons Daily) of portable water is available from the aquifer at the Big River site at a fraction of the cost of a new reservoir.

Therefore, as a result of the above actions and reasons stated the Project is de facto abandoned.

Chapter 7 – Decade of the 1990's
Law Suits, Questionable Practices

The 1990's

- **Class action lawsuit won and then lost (but could be brought back!)**

- **General Assembly passes unconstitutional law**

- **Future development prohibited except for special interests**

In 1990 former landowners brought suit against the State of Rhode Island to get their land back represented by Attorney Arlene Violet. Judge Gagnon dismissed the suit without prejudice, meaning it can be renewed if the reservoir is not built in a timely fashion.

The following is from the class action lawsuit filed by attorneys Arlene Violet & Robert Kiernan filed in superior court C.A. No 91-2900June 20, 1991. The plaintiffs were George Lemaire, Frank Lemaire, Alice Lavigne, Estate of Wilfred Lemaire, Lawrence Conti, Josephine Conti and Belnira Sacramento a/k/a Bella Sacramento, Cecile Tellier, and Marion L. Piaczyk. VS Water Resources Board a/k/a Water Resources Coordinating Board.

Excerpts from the lawsuit made the following statements:

- *For approximately 24 years the defendant has unsuccessfully attempted to implement the Big River Reservoir project, so-called.*
- *The project has been turned down finally by the United States Environmental Protection Agency....*
- *There is no reasonable likelihood that the sites will*

be used in the reasonable foreseeable future for the intended purpose for which the defendant was authorized to secure it.

- *The defendant has already spoiled the land entrusted to it.*
- *The defendant is unable to perform and/or to use the property.*
- *The U.S. House of Representatives and the U.S. Senate DE authorized the project, and the President of the United States confirmed such DE authorization on or about December, 1990.*
- *The project is, de facto, abandoned.*
- *Under the Rhode Island and United States constitutions, the respective statutes herein, and the common law, the plaintiffs are entitled to a riveter of the land, and the defendant is violating the rights of the plaintiffs by refusing to return said land.*

In 1993, the Rhode Island General Assembly passed the following Act in Chapter 220 RIGL, 37-20-1 Big River Reservoir – DEVELOPMENT PROHIBITED!!! "All lands acquired by the State or any subdivision thereof for the development of the "Rig River Reservoir" so called RIGL 1964 Chapter 133 shall not be sold nor shall the land be developed in any way. **The State shall not allow any future development or continued development of such property, and said property shall be designed "open space" as defined in RIGL 45-36-1**

The author believes the General Assembly acted unconstitutionally and deprived some of its Citizens their property rights. What "Public Use" can "open space" serve? If we allow this to continue none of our own property is safe from governmental seizures for non-public use under the auspices of "Eminent Domain."

Should PRIVATE PROPERTY be taken by EMINENT DOMAIN for OPEN SPACE?

Rhode Island General Law – Chapter 20 "Big River Reservoir Moratorium" section 37-20-1

37-20-1 **Big River Reservoir – Development prohibited**. *- All land acquired by the state or any subdivision thereof for the development of the 'Big River Reservoir" so-called, including any land acquired by the Big River – Wood River Reservoir Site Acquisition Act, P.L. 1964, ch. 133, shall not be sold nor shall the land be developed in any way. The state shall not allow any future development or continued development on that property, and the property shall be designated "open space" as defined in 45-36-1(1)-(7).*

Provided, however, that the foregoing shall not be construed to prohibit the use of the said property as a water reservoir and in the event an appropriate state agency makes a determination, then it shall not require legislative action to remove the property from "open space" as defined in 45-36-1(1)-(8).

The NO DEVELOPMENT rules were broken.

In 2003 the Hopkins Hill Sand and Stone LLC was allowed to pave a NEW asphalt road through approximately 2 miles of reservoir land approved by the RI Water Resources division citing safety issues. Also, electrical utility upgrades and various new buildings were constructed within the reservoir property.

In 2003, the Amgen Corp was allowed to pave a NEW parking lot, planted trees and erected fences in approximately 2 acres of the reservoir property, which was later totally removed.

Various politicians also attempted to get a bond to build a new State police barracks in the reservoir property that never materialized but was considered WHAT

DEVELOPMENT IS NEXT for the Big River Reservoir property?

Are State Laws for everyone or should exemptions be allowed?

In July, 1997 the RI Water Resources Board published a 9 page document titled, *"BIG RIVER MANAGEMENT AREA POLICIES."*

I am providing the full text of the document as Appendix A in the back of this book to more clearly define its merits both pro and con.

Legislator Tries to Get Study Commission

The 2000's

- **Study Commission approved by the General Assembly**

- **Members never appointed to the Commission by the House Sneaker!?**

In 2002, I was elected as State Representative from Coventry District 28.

As a new freshman Legislator, I had several priorities: cutting State sales and income taxes; regionalization of police and fire districts; consolidation of our 39 school districts and of course the Big River Reservoir project.

I submitted legislation to create a "Big River Reservoir" study commission. I was one of only thirteen Republicans in the Democratic controlled General Assembly consisting of 75 members. I was able to have my study commission approved by the house on two separate occasions. However, the then house Speaker William Murphy never appointed me or any of my suggested colleagues to the official commission. I sent several written requests to make appointment to the Speaker and even though I was personally told the appointments were forthcoming, they never happened. It's a shame the study commission was never assembled. It could have been vetted the entire project and possibly made good recommendations bring final closure to the 239 families who were affected by the floored Eminent Domain policy.

We did however have a few discussions of the project on the House floor when it came up for voting. During my time as State Representative 2002 – 2008, I was also a member of the House finance committee. As a member, I oversaw the budgets of the DOT (Department of Transportation) and the DEM (Department of Environmental Management. I had several opportunities to question the DEM on its practices in the Big River management area, and I did ask many tough questions.

Chapter 9 – Decade of the 2010's
No Reservoir; How About Deep Wells?

It has been nearly 50 years since the acquisition of the Big River land was authorized. 50 years of the land sitting dormant, 50 years of economic development that has not taken place because some of the most valuable real estate in Rhode Island has been owned by the state. Land controlled not by the private citizens to whom it rightfully belongs, and who could have made good use of it, but by an uncaring and inefficient state government.

239 families had the homes and land confiscated for a reservoir that will never be built.

The current estimated costs to construct a reservoir now are about 1 Billion? With NO federal funding Rhode Island in its current poor economic condition could **NEVER** afford to build a reservoir on its own.

It is now clear that the predicted water shortage which precipitated the Big River project never materialized. If such a crisis did occur, several deep water wells could be dug to resolve the issue. Of course, the State would not need to own 8,000 acres of land for a handful of deep water wells. A far better solution would be for individual landowners to grant easements on their property for these wells if they were in fact necessary. This is not an idle suggestion, the idea is currently being investigated by several state agencies However, even for this project, which is relatively inexpensive compared to the original reservoir proposal, has no funding and is unlikely to get any. Not a drop of water has come out of the Rig River in nearly 50 years!

As the story continues today and is still being written without closure, I wonder what would it be like if the Big River property was never taken and also what would the future of this land look like? Back in 1964 interstate Route 95 was being built in Rhode Island, making the Big River Reservoir property one of the most valuable commercial real estate in the northeast. About 75 miles from Boston and about 125 miles to New York great location for development and potential tax revenue for local communities and the State of Rhode Island. The recent Center of New England development project in Coventry situated along Route 95's westerly border proves how valuable this property really is. With WalMart, Home Depot, and BJ's as anchors along with several restaurants, a nursing home and residential complex....a goldmine for the developers and tax revenue for the town Coventry and the State of Rhode Island. Of course hundreds of new jobs were also created. One can only imagine what the easterly side of Route 95 stretching from the town of East Greenwich to the town of Exeter approximately 5 miles along the northeast corridor that connects Florida to Maine. Consider how much the local communities have lost in tax revenue over the past 50 years....**MILLIONS!!!** Think about how much more these towns will lose in tax revenue in the future....**MILLIONS** more if the land stays in "Open Space".

Entrance to Carrs Pond Trail
West Greenwich
Located within Big RiverArea

Chapter 10
The Future and the What-If Scenario

As I conclude this book the future of the Big River Reservoir still is totally unclear and the land use remains in "Open Space". I hope someday the 239 families will get their land back and this unfortunate ordeal will end for them. Hopefully, there are others who like me will continue to fight against unjust eminent domain violations. When one person is unjustly treated and no one cares, who will come to your aid if you are next?

Finally, I often wonder what if the State of Rhode Island and Providence Plantations decided not to take the Big River land back in the early 1960's, what would this section of Rhode Island look like today? Certainly the northerly boundary of Route 95 would be fully developed from the East Greenwich to Exeter. The population of West Greenwich would be greater; the Town would be richer with more commercial development and increased tax revenue. **West Greenwich would be the true Center of New England!**

What Can You Do?

To help the original families and their next-of-kin get their land back I will set up a bank account for legal fees to bring their case back to court at the Coventry Credit Union. I will donate all profits of this book to that fund.

Big River Families Legal Fund

Appendix A

Source:
http://www.wrb.ri.gov/policy_guidelines_brmalanduse/BRMA_Policies.pdf

RI WATER RESOURCES BOARD

BIG RIVER MANAGEMENT AREA

POLICIES

July 1997

AUTHORITY: These regulations are adopted in accordance with Chapter 42-35 pursuant to Chapter 46-8 of the Rhode Island General Laws, as amended.

TABLE OF CONTENTS

PREFACE

The following policies have been developed to guide the Rhode Island Water Resources Board in its management of the state-owned property in the Big River Management Area. It recognizes the natural resources of the area and those public uses that are compatible with them. The plan addresses administration, operation, maintenance and development requirements as well as the budgetary demands imposed.

The Board further recognizes the present usage of the land by the original owners. Only by joint local and state concern for the natural features of the area can the character of the region be maintained. The Board also acknowledges that all aquifers within the State must be preserved. The Big River Management Area is a water aquifer under State control and the integrity of the water quality can and must be preserved.

Furthermore, the RI Water Resources Board is committed to providing equal opportunity in every aspect of its programs and will not discriminate because of race, sex, national origin, age, religion, sexual orientation, or disability.

Acknowledgments

The RI Water Resources Board wishes to thank all persons who were instrumental in the development of the Big River Policy Book as well as all those who live within, or contribute to the daily operations of the Big River Management Area.

Administration

The Big River Reservoir concept was initiated in 1928. It was not until 1962 that a Special Governor's Commission recommended acquisition of the property. In 1964, the General Assembly, under the Big River-Wood River Acquisition Act, established a requirement for a bond issue of five million dollars ($5,000,000) to be placed on the general referendum ballot. Having recently experienced the inconveniences and health hazard associated with several drought seasons, the voters passed the bond referendum.

Under the powers of eminent domain, the state began acquiring property by condemnation beginning in Coventry in 1965, West Greenwich in 1966, and the in the Wood River area in Exeter in 1967. Due to substantial litigation, both the amount of land and the cost of acquisition exceeded desired proportions. In the end, the state obtained a total of 8,600 acres from 351 owners which comprised 444 parcels at a cost of $7.5 million. Management of the land and the 200 structures thereon, became the responsibility of the Water Resources Coordinating Board, forerunner of the Water Resources Board.

Due to the opposition to the reservoir by the federal government, the US Environmental Protection Agency, and environmental organizations, the state placed the project on indefinite hold in 1990. In 1993, the RI General Assembly passed legislation declaring the Big River Management Area as "Open Space," to be utilized and enjoyed by residents of the State of Rhode Island. To this end, several civic groups engage in activities ranging from sports, hiking, canoeing, military training and other recreational activities.

JURISDICTION AND RESPONSIBILITY

RI General Laws 1956, Chapter 46-15-6, Powers and Duties. In order to implement the plans and programs, the Board shall have the following powers and duties in addition to those powers enumerated under Chapter 46-15.1-5:

(a)   To acquire, with the limitation of funds therefore, the sites, appurtenant marginal lands, dams, waters, water rights, rights-of-way, easements, and other property or interests in property for reservoirs, ground water wells, well sites, and for such pipe lines, aqueducts, pumping stations, filtration plants and auxiliary structures as may be necessary or desirable for the treatment and distribution of water from those reservoirs, ground water wells and well sites. Lands acquired under the provisions of this section shall be acquired with the approval of the governor by purchase, gift device, or otherwise on such terms and conditions as the Board shall determine, or by the exercise of eminent domain, in accordance with the provisions of RIGL Chapter 6 of Title 37, as amended, insofar as the same are consistent with the provisions hereof;

2

51

(b)   To enter into contracts and/or agreements with such departments, divisions, agencies, or boards of the state as are directed by the governor to regulate, manage, or perform related functions of any lands or waters acquired under the provisions of the Big River-Wood River Reservoir Site Acquisition Act. (P.L. of 1964, Chapter 133);

(c)   To compensate the departments, divisions, agencies, or Board from the Water Development Fund established in RIGL Chapter 46-15.1-20 in an amount equal to the cost of providing such functions or services as are directed to be performed by the governor. The compensation shall be mandatory and shall be provided according to procedures established by the RI Department of Administration.

RI Public Law 1964, Chapter 133, Section 7 . . . the water resources co-ordinating board . . . Said Bard is vested with all power and authority necessary or incidental to the purposes of this act. When deemed necessary, the Board reserves the right to authorize the State Police, RI Department of Environmental Management, and the RI National Guard, Air and Ground Divisions to perform duties on behalf of the Board.

FACILITIES

Of the 200 buildings taken at the time of condemnation, there remained 47 residential homes, 79 mobile homes, 3 commercial buildings and a 9-hole golf course. In addition, there is a Field Office, located at 612 Nooseneck Hill Road, West Greenwich, which is the base of operations in the Big River Management Area.

EQUIPMENT

In conjunction with the Memorandum of Understanding with the RI National Guard, the Board has at its disposal the following equipment: front-end loaders, high utility motion vehicles, bulldozers, water tankers, 4x4 trucks, graders, various hand tools and manpower.

POLICIES

In the operation of the Big River Management Area, the Board, having taken into consideration comments voiced at a public hearing, adopted the following policies, which have been filed with the Secretary of State. Specific agreements related to these policies are on file at the Water Resources Board office.

3

POLICY CONCERNING USE OF THE BIG RIVER MANAGEMENT AREA

Consistent with the General Assembly designation of the Big River Management Area as open space to be utilized and enjoyed by residents of the State of Rhode Island, the Water Resources Board may allow individual and organized recreational and training activities within the area. Groups and/or organizations interested in conducting such activities must submit a Big River Management Area Land Use Request Form to the Board thirty (30) days prior to the activity date. The Board requires verification of general liability insurance coverage in an amount determined by the Board and/or reserves the right to require additional information it deems necessary. Individual activities which do not require Board approval include, but are not limited to, hunting, fishing, hiking, canoeing of Big River and horseback riding. Activities that are forbidden include swimming, trapping, camping, off-road biking, clear-cutting, firewood cutting and canoeing on ponds. Fuel, electric motors and all terrain vehicles are forbidden in the Big River Management Area. The Board will seek the assistance of local and state law enforcement agencies in the removal/detainment of persons found engaging in unauthorized activities within the Big River Management Area. The Board cannot be held liable for any injuries sustained during voluntary recreational use of the Big River Management Area.

POLICY CONCERNING FAIR MARKET APPRAISALS

In order to maintain rental market comparability on the Big River Management Area rental properties, the Water Resources Board will complete an initial fair market rental appraisal, using a comparative approach. The fair market rents established by this appraisal process will be reviewed annually. The housing component of the Consumer Price Index (CPI) for the New England Region, effective the preceding year, will be utilized to determine the annual rental increase. Notification of the rental increase will be provided to the tenants during the month of May with an effective rent increase on July 1 of that year. The Board will conduct subsequent fair market rental appraisals of all residential and commercial Big River Management Area properties on the fifth anniversary year commencing 1995, 2000, 2005, etc.

POLICY ON RENTAL FREEZE FOR ORIGINAL OWNERS & SENIOR CITIZENS ON 1977 LIST

In 1977, the Water Resources Board and State Property Committee met to review and establish the rent for various Big River properties condemned and taken into state ownership. With input from state and local officials, the decision was made to "freeze" the rent charged to those individuals whose property was condemned for the Big River Reservoir but who continued to live there as tenants of the Water Resources Board. These "original owners" are defined as those persons whose names appear on the original deed and lease agreements signed in 1964 at the time of the land condemnation. This rent concession is exclusive to the original owner(s) of the premises while he or she is a tenant of the Water Resources Board in that home which he or she owned at the time of condemnation. The rent concession shall terminate upon the death of the

4

original owner or if the original owner fails to reside on a continuous and uninterrupted basis at the premises or upon termination of tenancy for breach or nonpayment. This rent concession will not apply to family members of the original owner and cannot be assigned or transferred.

Senior Citizens over sixty-five who resided on Big River properties in 1977 were also granted a "freeze" in rent. This stabilized rent concession is exclusive to the senior citizen tenants who resided on the Big River property in 1977. This rent concession shall terminate upon death of the tenant or if the senior citizen fails to reside on a continuous and uninterrupted basis at the premises or upon the termination of tenancy for breach or nonpayment. This rent concession cannot be assigned or transferred.

POLICY CONCERNING SUBLEASING BY ALL TENANTS OTHER THAN ORIGINAL OWNERS

No tenants of the Big River Management Area are authorized to sublease any portion of the leased property, residences or other buildings located on or about his or her property, with the only exception being the one currently existing sublease for which the Board is presently scheduled to render a formal approval. Failure of the tenant to comply with this policy and the lease agreement is a default of the lease agreement with the Board. Upon default by a tenant, the Board will begin eviction proceedings as set forth under state law.

Original Owners, who currently have Board approval, may extend the sublease to their property only after submitting a request to the Water Resources Board and receiving Board approval. The sublease request will set forth the actual intended sub-lessee's uses, insurance of the sub-lessee, any financial agreements between the lessee and sub-lessee. The Board reserves the right to request any additional information it deems appropriate prior to the ruling on the lessee's sublease request.

POLICY CONCERNING TEMPORARY REDUCED RENT FOR LOW INCOME TENANTS

The Big River property is not subsidized housing. However, the Board recognizes that certain existing tenants in the Big River Management Area do not have sufficient financial resources to lease the property they currently occupy at the fair market price. Therefore, in accord with guidelines established by US Housing and Urban Development, the Board will allow qualified existing tenants to remit no more than 30 percent (30%) of their household income for rent, effective on the signing of the new lease agreement. These tenants shall complete income verification forms provided by the Board to substantiate claims of inability to pay fair market rent. Tenants will be required to update household income information on an annual basis and/or upon any change of circumstances in household income or family status. Providing false or incomplete information relative to income will eliminate the tenant from eligibility for this program. Tenants participating in this program shall apply for subsidized housing to the local

5

housing authority or other housing agency at the time of application to this program and will provide copies of the same to the Board. The concern of the Water Resources Board is to insure that no existing tenant is displaced, due to inability to pay the fair market rent. However this program is temporary in nature and is not intended to supply permanent subsidized housing. Only those persons who are Big River tenants as of December 1, 2000 are eligible to participate in this program. This program shall terminate on December 31, 2005.

POLICY CONCERNING INSPECTIONS

In order to sustain a safe, habitable environment for its tenants, the Water Resources Board shall conduct inspections no less than once a year of the residential and commercial facilities located within the Big River Management Area. Said inspections will be performed by the State Building Code Commission or other state-approved entity which will report any findings of State Building Code violations to the Water Resources Board. The findings of the inspection shall be deemed conclusive to the condition of the property. In the event the dwelling is deemed irreparable and/or condemned by the State Building Code Inspector or other entity, the Water Resources Board reserves the right to terminate the lease and begin eviction proceedings. All buildings so designated will be razed as soon after the vacancy as practicable.

POLICY ON MAINTENANCE RESPONSIBILITIES

Recognizing the responsibility of the tenant to maintain their dwelling as follows: The tenant agrees during the continuance of the lease to keep the interior and exterior of the leased Premises leased in good repair, ordinary wear and tear excepted, including the setting of glass in windows and doors, if any, and in addition thereto, the Tenant covenants and agrees to maintain the heating, plumbing, electrical, and all other mechanical and structural systems and to repair any damage caused by Tenant's misuse of all appliances within the leased Premises, including but without limiting the generality thereof: the plumbing facilities, heating appliances, electrical wires and fixtures, if any. The Tenant will indemnify, defend and save harmless the Landlord from any and all loss or damage which at any time during the continuance of this lease may be caused to anyone or anything by the leakage or escape of any water to the leased Premises which is in any way caused by the Tenant. At the expiration, or sooner termination of this lease, Tenant shall quietly and peacefully surrender up to the Landlord full possession of the leased Premises together with all improvements, alterations and additions made during the term of the lease by either Tenant or Landlord, all in as good order as they now are or may be put in. The tenant agrees to repair any holes in floors, walls and fixtures of the Leased Premises caused by Tenant, and in the event that said Tenant shall leave the leased Premises in such a condition that Landlord shall be required to repair or restore the leased Premises, Tenant agrees, upon demand of Landlord, to pay the cost and expense thereof. The Water Resources Board has reduced the fair market rent value of each dwelling by an amount which reflects the average cost of maintaining the property in good condition in the standard set forth in the State Building Code. The Board will determine the rent reduction amount based upon recommendation of a licensed appraiser. No structural alterations shall be made unless the Lessee first obtains the permission in writing from the Water Resources Board using the "Request for Maintenance Form." Failure of the tenant to maintain and/or repair the property is a default of the lease agreement with the Board. Upon default by a tenant, the Board will begin eviction proceedings as set forth under state law.

POLICY ON APPLICATION PROCESS

The process for applying for property rental within the Big River Management Area shall be as follows:

1. Application will be made available at the Water Resources Board Field Office, 612 Nooseneck Hill Road, West Greenwich, or other address designated by the Board, and will be provided by mail, upon request;

2. Applicants must complete Application Form and provide verification of employment as well as rent history from a prior/present landlord(s).

3. Board staff will review the application and determine acceptability based on number of occupants, household income and information provided by prior/present landlord(s).

4. Applicants will be notified by mail of determination of acceptance/refusal and in the case of acceptance, the position on the waiting list.

Accepted applicants will be placed on a waiting list based on the official date of application, i.e., the date received by the Big River Management Area Property Manager. Applicants must complete a Notice of Continued Interest in Leasing Property form on an annual basis. Failure to complete this form will result in the applicant's name being removed from the waiting list. Applicants will be placed in available homes based on application date and suitability of home relative to the number of occupants.

POLICY ON HAZARDOUS MATERIALS

The RI Water Resources Board prohibits storage within the Big River Management Area of any listed hazardous substances in a quantity greater that the final reportable quantities as specified in 40 CFR 302.4, Superfund Hazardous Materials List. Furthermore, all commercial tenants are to comply with RIGL 28-21, Hazardous Substance Right-To-Know Law. A copy of both the law and regulation are on file at the Water Resources Board Field Office, 612 Nooseneck Hill Road, West Greenwich. Failure by a tenant to adhere to this policy will be considered a breach of the lease agreement; subsequently the Board may initiate eviction proceedings as set forth under state law.

POLICY CONCERNING CATASTROPHIC REPAIRS

The RI Water Resources Board, on each situation, will determine the requirements and procedures for repair of catastrophic damages. On behalf of the Board, the State Building Inspector or an authorized agent will inspect the property and advise the Board as to the extent of the repair necessary. The Board will approve the actions to be taken consistent with the opinion of the State Building Inspector and in accord with the mandates of the Rhode Island General Laws which may include repair, or demolition of, the building when appropriate.

PROTECTION

The Water Resources Board employs the assistance of local and state emergency personnel. The Mishnock Fire Company provides coverage for the area inclusive of Hopkins Hill Road, Division Road, Burnt Sawmill Road and Nooseneck Hill Road (up to Big River Bridge). The West Greenwich Fire Company supports the remainder of the Big River Management Area. The area is also patrolled by the RI Dept. of Environmental Management's Enforcement Division Conservation officers.

HISTORICAL SITES

The Water Resources Board intends to coordinate with the RI Historical Preservation Society for the possible relocation of several historical homes within the Big River Management Area, prior to demolition, major renovation or initiation of construction of the Big River Reservoir. The Board also intends to relocate several historical cemeteries as part of the reservoir project. With the exception of the Hopkins Cemetery, these cemeteries are no longer functional. On April 24, 1978, the Board granted Ardis Barbour permission to be buried in her family cemetery on Hopkins Hill Road. This particular cemetery is located on high ground and will not be relocated due to the reservoir construction.

REVENUE

RI General Law 1956, Chapter 46-15.1-20 Water development account fund. (a) There is hereby created a special fund called "water development fund" from any net proceeds which may be paid to the state as a result of the lease of any reservoir sites or other facilities as may be acquired or constructed by the state in accordance with the provisions of this chapter and chapter 15.1 of this title, as amended, or as otherwise authorized or permitted, or as a result of the sale of surplus property or any interest therein, including without limiting the generality of the foregoing, the sale of excess gravel, timber or tother materials located on the reservoir sites or other facilities. Monies from this fund are hereby appropriated for the purposes authorized by

Chapter 46-15-6 and also hereby made available for borrowing by the board, in accordance with and pursuant to the provisions of Chapter 46-15.1-4, exclusive of acquisition of reservoir sites, and the state controller is hereby authorized and directed to draw his or her orders upon the general treasurer for the payment or loan of such sums or such portions thereof as may be required from time to time upon receipt by him of properly authenticated vouchers; provided, however, that in the event the water development account created by this chapter exceeds the sum of one million dollars ($1,000,000) such excess over that amount is hereby made available and appropriated for expenditure by the board to implement the plans and programs thereof as are authorized by this chapter and chapter 15.1 of this title, the general laws exclusive of the acquisition of reservoir sites.

9

About the Author

Victor George. Moffitt was born on February 2, 1950 in West Warwick at the Mitchell Maternity. Victor grew up living on Hopkins Hill Rd. in West Greenwich and attended the West Greenwich Elementary School (currently named the Lineham School). Victor was a boy scout in Troop 35 Lake Mishnock (Star scout). Victor attended Coventry High School and graduated in 1968 (there was no high school in West Greenwich at the time). He joined the US Air Force and served for four years and spend one year in Vietnam.

Married in 1972 to Bertha Wolf, he is a father of four Kevin, Brian, Melanie and Mary. He is a grandfather of nine and his one great grandson.

He attended Johnson & Wales University and has a bachelor's degree in Accounting. He started Victor Moffitt & Co. Inc. bookkeeping and tax practice in 1972; his daughter Mary joined the firm in 2001. Victor also started Moffitt & Associates, LLC in 2001 an independent financial services company specializing in financial planning and investments.

He was elected to the RI General Assembly in 2002 as a State Representative from Coventry District 28 and served 3 terms until he retired in 2008. As a State Rep he served on House Finance and Veteran Affairs committees. He earned a CWS (Certified Wealth Strategist) designation in 2010 from Cannon Financial Institute. Victor was also past commander of the Coventry/West Greenwich VFW and member of the Coventry West Greenwich Elks, Coventry AMVETS and Club Jocques.

He is an avid chess player and member of the **USCF**. He also enjoys playing guitar at Church and golf with family and friends.

Will this be the end

of the road

for the 239 families

or will you help?

You can help by sending a donation (not tax deductible) to the

"Big River Families Legal Fund"

c/o Victor Moffitt

1260 Main St. Coventry, RI 02816